Traveling on a Train

2-D Shapes

Suzanne Barchers

Publishing Credits

Dona Herweck Rice, *Editor-in-Chief*; Lee Aucoin, *Creative Director*; Don Tran, *Print Production Manager*; Sara Johnson, *Senior Editor*; Jamey Acosta, *Associate Editor*; Neri Garcia, *Interior Layout Designer*; Stephanie Reid, *Photo Editor*; Rachelle Cracchiolo, M.A.Ed., *Publisher*

Image Credits

cover Kentoh/Shutterstock; p.1 Kentoh/Shutterstock; p.5 Holger Mette/Shutterstock; p.6 Dan Breckwoldt/Shutterstock; p.7 Brian Weed/Shutterstock; p.8 Achauer/Dreamstime; p.9 Chad Mcdermott/Dreamstime; p.10 (top) Dominique Landau/Shutterstock, (bottom left) Risteski Goce/Shutterstock, (bottom right) Oculo/Shutterstock; p.12 amolmd/BigStockPhoto; p.11 aka Kath/Flickr; p.13 Robert Pernell/Shutterstock; p.14 Fotohunter/Shutterstock; p.15 (top) Marcin Okupniak/Dreamstime, (bottom) Geoff Pickering/BigStockPhoto; p.16 SFC/BigStockPhoto; p.17 OPLA/Shutterstock; p.18 Dino O./Shutterstock; p.19 (left) Susan Law Cain/Shutterstock, (right) IOfoto/Shutterstock; p.20 Bruce Shippee/Shutterstock; p.21 (top) Robert Crow/Shutterstock, (middle) Jason Maehl/Shutterstock, (bottom) Clearviewstock /Shutterstock; p.22 (top) Luminouslens/Shutterstock, (bottom) Panoramic Images/Getty Images; p.23 Rieteree/Flickr; p.24 (top) Pfistner Photography/BigStockPhoto, (bottom) Sam Diesel/iStockphoto; p.25 Vidiot/Flickr; p.26 Bitchcake/Flickr; p.27 Magnus/Flickr; p.28 Tim Bradley

Teacher Created Materials

5301 Oceanus Drive
Huntington Beach, CA 92649-1030
http://www.tcmpub.com
ISBN 978-0-7439-0869-6
© 2011 Teacher Created Materials, Inc.
Reprinted 2013

Table of Contents

Shapes All Around

There are many different shapes in the world. Some shapes are **two-dimensional**. That means the shape has a length and a width. Two-dimensional shapes also have sides. Some have **vertices**. Vertices are the points where sides meet.

Two-dimensional shapes can be seen when you travel. Trains and train stations are filled with interesting two-dimensional shapes. So climb aboard for a shape-seeing adventure!

Starting Your Trip at Los Angeles's Union Station

All aboard! Those words tell you that it is time to start your train trip. But you have a few things to do before you go.

The clocks on the clock tower are the first **circles** you see at Union Station in Los Angeles. Be sure you have extra time. You will want to look around this station.

Circles do not have vertices, but they are two-dimensional shapes. The distance from the center of the circle to the edge is the same all the way around.

Look up when you get inside. The **designer** loved shapes. Count how many circles you can see. Look again. What other shapes can you find?

Look down and you will find more circles inside of circles. The floor is covered in **triangles**, too.

A triangle is a flat shape with 3 sides. The points where the sides meet are called vertices.

A triangle always has 3 vertices. Look at these shapes. Then answer the questions.

1.  2. 3.

a. How many vertices are in shape 1?

b. How many vertices are in shape 2?

c. How many vertices are in shape 3?

d. Which shapes are triangles? How do you know?

As you board the train, you may get to see the train's wheels. The wheels must be perfectly round to travel safely at high speeds.

LET'S EXPLORE MATH

Which of these shapes are circles? How do you know?

1.

2.

3.

4.

Stopping in Chicago's Union Station

Get off the train at Chicago's Union Station. Look up at the **squares**! A square has 4 sides. Each side is the same length. The sides are **parallel**, too. That means the 2 lines are always the same distance apart.

Look at the station from the outside. The upper windows are squares, too.

A square is a flat shape with 4 sides. The sides are all equal in length. The points where the sides meet are called vertices. Look at these shapes. Then answer the questions.

1.   2.   3.

a. How many vertices are in shape 1?

b. How many vertices are in shape 2?

c. How many vertices are in shape 3?

d. Which shape is a square? How do you know?

Train tracks have rails and ties.
The ties are the shorter pieces under
the rails. The rails are parallel. The
ties are parallel, too.

The ties are **rectangles**.
A rectangle has 4 sides
and 4 vertices. There
are 2 short sides that are
parallel. There are 2 long
sides that are parallel.

Really long parallel lines look like they meet when you look at them from the ground. But they still look parallel from high above.

1.

2.

3.

Which set of lines shows parallel lines?

Watch as you leave the station. You might see a turntable in the train yard. The first train engines ever made could not back up. The train would drive onto a huge turntable to turn around.

A turntable is one big circle. Train engines would get repaired in a big building near the turntable. The building is called a roundhouse.

You might see open freight cars full of coal or grain on your trip. Do you see the rectangular shape of these box cars? The box cars can hold all kinds of freight.

 LET'S EXPLORE MATH

Look at these shapes. Which of the shapes are rectangles? How do you know?

1.   2.   3.   4.

Years ago, you might have seen milk trains. They stopped often to pick up and deliver milk. What shapes do you see on this old train?

Look through the rectangular windows on your trip. You can pass the time watching for shapes on railroad signs.

This is called a crossbuck sign. It is used at railroad crossings. Find the rectangles on it.

Stopping in Washington D.C. and Philadelphia

Get off the train at Union Station in Washington, D.C. You may feel like you are walking through circles. Look closely at the ceiling. You will find lots of squares, triangles, and rectangles.

Can you find the shape with eight sides? That shape is called an **octagon**. Do not miss the floor either. The designer loved using shapes!

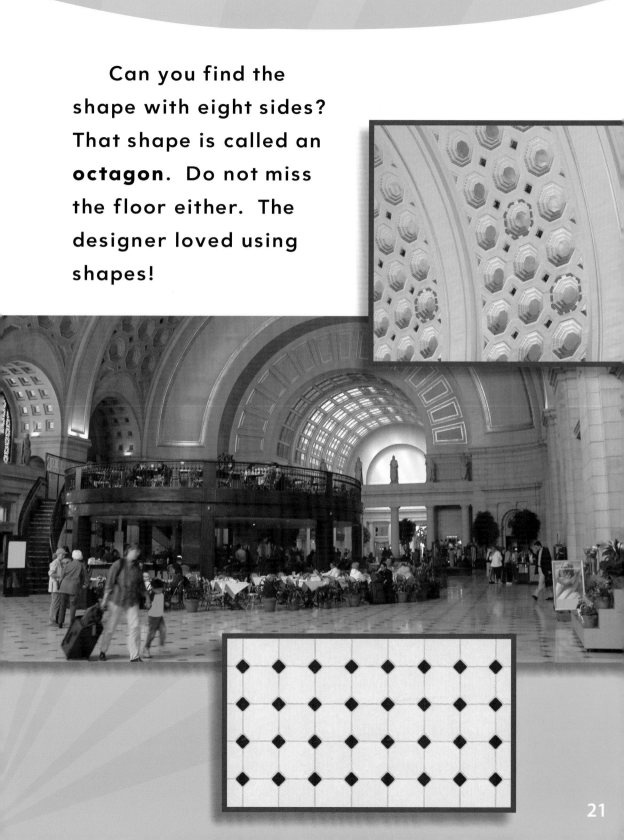

Welcome to Philadelphia! There are so many things to see and do here. First look around the 30th Street Station. The designer loved squares and rectangles.

Look at the ceiling. You will see squares inside of squares. Then look at the windows. You will see rows of rectangles. Even the lights have rectangles, squares, and an octagon!

Last Stop! New York City's Grand Central Station

Your last stop is New York City! Grand Central Station has its share of shapes, too. You can also see constellations on the ceiling.

The ceiling was dirty for many years.
Look up. You will see one area that
shows how dirty the ceiling used to be.
What shape is the dirty spot?

There is one more thing to do before you end your trip. Find the whispering gallery. First, take a look at all those rectangles.

Then stand in one corner. Have a friend stand in the opposite corner. Then whisper something. The rounded ceiling will take your whispers right to your friend. It can be your little secret!

Train Shapes

Shapes are found in many places and on many things. This is a drawing of a train that was used in the 1800s. Can you find all the shapes in the drawing?

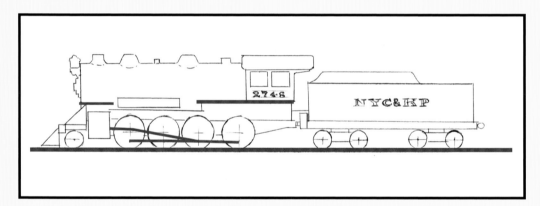

a. How many circles are in the drawing?

b. How many triangles are in the drawing?

c. How many squares are in the drawing?

d. How many rectangles are in the drawing?

e. How many shapes are there in total?

Solve It!

Use the steps below to help you solve the problems.

Step 1: Start at the left. Count all the circles from left to right. Write how many circles you counted.

Step 2: Repeat Step 1 and count all the triangles. Write how many triangles you counted.

Step 3: Start on the left again. This time, look for squares. Write how many squares you counted.

Step 4: Start on the left again. Look for rectangles first in the locomotive. Be careful! Some are very small. Then count the rectangles in the freight car. Write how many rectangles you counted.

Step 5: To find the total, add up all the shapes you counted.

Glossary

circles—flat, round shapes

designer—a person who creates a plan or drawing for something

octagon—a flat shape with 8 sides

parallel—lines that are the same distance apart and never overlap

rectangles—flat shapes with 4 vertices and 2 different sets of equal parallel sides

squares—flat shapes with 4 vertices and 4 equal sides

triangles—flat shapes with 3 sides and 3 vertices

two-dimensional—a flat shape that has both length and width

vertices—the points where 2 or more sides meet

Index

Let's Explore Math

Page 9:

a. 3 vertices

b. 3 vertices

c. 4 vertices

d. Shapes 1 and 2 are triangles; answers will vary, but should include that triangles have 3 vertices or 3 sides.

Page 10:

Shapes in 1 and 3 are circles; answers will vary, but should include that circles are the same distance from the center all the way around.

Page 12:

a. 4 vertices

b. 4 vertices

c. 4 vertices

d. Shape 2; answers will vary, but should include that all 4 sides are equal.

Page 14:

The lines in 2 are parallel.

Page 17:

Shapes 1, 2, and 3 are rectangles; answers will vary, but should include that rectangles have 4 vertices and 4 sides that are parallel.

Solve the Problem

Answers will vary for all problems.